Money

Margaret Hall

Heinemann
LIBRARY

www.heinemann.co.uk/library
Visit our website to find out more information about Heinemann Library books.

To order:
 Phone 44 (0)1865 888066
 Send a fax to 44 (0)1865 314091
 Visit the Heinemann Bookshop at www.heinemann.co.uk/library to browse our catalogue and order online.

Heinemann Library is an imprint of **Pearson Education**, a company incorporated in England and Wales having its registered office at Edinburgh Gate, Harlow, Essex, CM20 2JE – Registered company number: 00872828

Heinemann is a registered trademark of Pearson Education Limited.

Text © Pearson Education Limited 2008
The moral rights of the proprietor have been asserted.

Edited by Charlotte Guillain and Catherine Veitch
Designed by Kim Miracle, Victoria Bevan and
    AMR Design Ltd
Illustrated by Mark Preston
Picture research by Hannah Taylor
Production: Victoria Fitzgerald

Originated by DOT Gradations Ltd
Printed and bound in China by Leo Paper Group

ISBN 978 0 4311 1681 5
12 11 10 09 08
10 9 8 7 6 5 4 3 2 1

British Library Cataloguing in Publication Data
Hall, Margaret
Money. - 2nd ed. - (Earning, saving, spending)
332.4
A full catalogue record for this book is available from the British Library.

Acknowledgements
We would like to thank the following for permission to reproduce photographs: ©Alamy pp. **4** (Mary Evans Picture Library), **7** (Rob Bartee), **8** (Julian Marshall), **22**, **23** (Gary Roebuck), **25** (PCL); ©Corbis pp. **5** (Nathan Benn), **18** (Charles O'Rear), **28** (William Whitehurst); ©Corbis Sygma p. **14**; ©Getty Images p. **29**; ©Pearson Education Ltd pp. **20** top left (Devon Obugenga Shaw), **20** top right (Gareth Boden), **20** bottom (Jules Selmes); ©Pearson Education Ltd/ Tudor Photography pp. **9**, **11**, **12**, **13**, **15** left, **15** right, **16**, **17**, **19**; ©The Art Archive p. **6** (Dagli Orti); ©Wishlist Images 2008 pp. **10**, **21**, **24** (Harry Rhodes).

Cover photograph of bundles of pound notes reproduced with permission of ©Corbis/ Steve Lupton.

Every effort has been made to contact copyright holders of material reproduced in this book. Any omissions will be rectified in subsequent printings if notice is given to the publishers.

Contents

Some words are shown in bold, **like this**. You can find out what they mean by looking in the glossary on page 30.

Before money

A long time ago, there was no money. People did not need any. They grew, gathered, or hunted for food. They built their own houses and made their own clothes. Sometimes people wanted things that other people had. A person who made beautiful pots might want a basket that another person made. So people would **barter**, or **trade**, with each other.

Hundreds of years ago, people bartered with each other, exchanging ideas and experiences as well as goods.

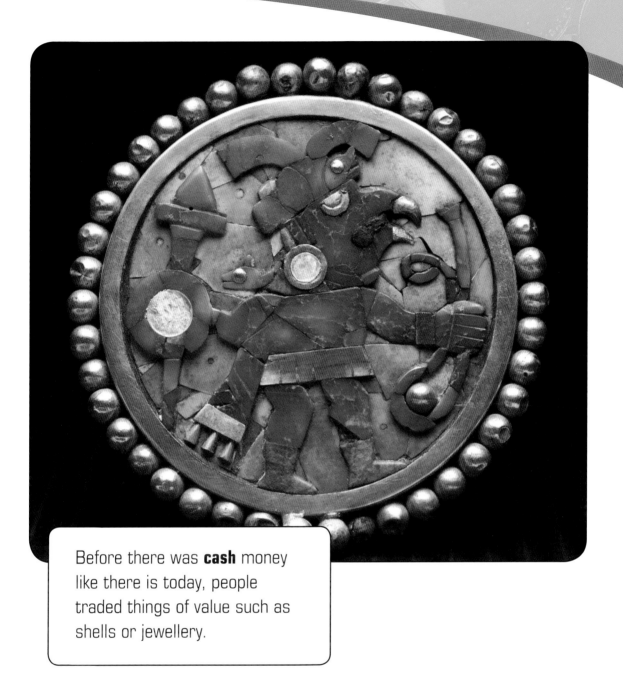

Before there was **cash** money like there is today, people traded things of value such as shells or jewellery.

Bartering worked most of the time. But sometimes people could not agree about what was fair. So they started to trade objects that were valuable to everyone. People used salt, grain, feathers, tea leaves, shells, beads, and even fish hooks in the same way we use money today.

The first money

Before using money, the ancient Egyptians traded things like wheat and barley in exchange for metals, animals, spices, and wood for building.

As time passed, people travelled further from home to **trade**. It was hard to carry things like salt and shells so someone had a better idea. Everyone agreed that metals such as gold and silver were valuable. So people started to use them for trade. They made the metal into bars, lumps, or circles. These circles were the first **coins**.

Before long, people all over the world used coins to trade for things. Many coins did not look like the ones we use today. But, like modern coins, they were easy to carry and had value.

Like today's coins, some coins from long ago had a picture of a **government** leader, king, or queen on them.

Money today

Today, most people do not **barter** for the things they need. They use money instead. **Coins** are still used, but today people also use paper money, or **banknotes**.

Today, people use coins and notes to buy the things they want.

The way money looks keeps changing. New coins and notes are made with different words and pictures on them. The materials people use to make money have changed, too. Coins today are made from a mixture of metals such as copper and nickel.

This is a range of **sterling** (British money) and euros, which are used in many European countries.

The value of money

Because money has value, people can exchange it for **goods** and **services**.

Coins and **banknotes** are not worth much by themselves. The metals and paper they are made of do not cost much. So, why do people think money is valuable?

Bank of England banknotes have the words 'promise to pay' written on them. They also have special features such as watermarks and holograms, so you know your money is the real thing. Fake banknotes are worthless. Everyone can trust the Bank's banknotes so they can use them to pay for things. The Bank of England is in charge of issuing most of the country's banknotes. Some banks in Scotland and Northern Ireland issue their own banknotes.

This is the Bank of England's promise to the person who has this note.

Coins

There are eight **coins** of different value used in the United Kingdom. How big a coin is does not tell you how much it is worth. A twenty-pence piece is smaller than a ten-pence piece, but it is worth more.

Sometimes special coins are made for important occasions, such as a royal wedding. Some coins are made especially for people to collect.

Coins come in different shapes, sizes, and colours so we can easily tell them apart. These are all the coins used in the United Kingdom.

These coins are euros, which are used in many European countries.

Coins are made at a **mint**. In the United Kingdom coins are made at the **Royal Mint**. The Royal Mint also makes coins for over 100 other countries, makes collectors' coins, and produces military medals. The Royal Mint started in small workshops in London, then it moved to the Tower of London. Today, the Royal Mint is in a modern factory.

Making coins

At a **mint**, the **coins** start out as a thin strip of metal. This metal is rolled until it is the right thickness and then a machine cuts the metal into circles, called blanks.

This machine is cutting blanks.

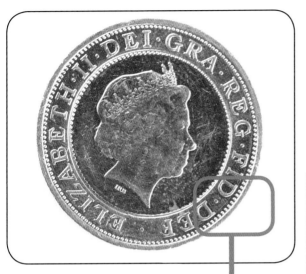

These are the two sides of a two-pound coin.

The writing is in **Latin**. It refers to the Queen, Elizabeth II.

This coin has a picture of a rose for England, and a thistle for Scotland.

The blanks travel to a machine that presses a design onto each side of them. In the United Kingdom one side of the coin always has the Queen's head on it. The other side has a different picture. There is writing on both sides of the coin and some coins also have writing around the edge.

Paper money

There are different kinds of paper money, or **banknotes**.
There are four different **Bank of England** banknotes – £5,
£10, £20, and £50. They are different sizes and colours
but they all have a picture of the Queen on them.

Bank of England banknotes show pictures of
famous British people from the past.

Paper money does not weigh much or take up much space. So, it is easier to carry than **coins**. A banknote is worth more than a coin, too. If a book costs five pounds, it is easy to pay for it with a five-pound note. It would take 500 one-pence pieces to pay for the same book!

A five-pound note is equal to 500 one-pence pieces. Sometimes, it is easier to carry banknotes than coins.

Making paper money

The **Bank of England's** banknotes are made at a factory in Essex. There are different designs for banknotes for England and Wales, Scotland, and Northern Ireland. Special paper and ink are used to make paper money. The paper starts with nothing on it. Then it goes through a machine called a **printing press** that puts words and pictures on both sides.

Paper money is printed in large sheets and then cut to make each banknote.

Serial numbers

BB39 052785

BB39 052785

Each banknote of the same value has many of the same words and pictures printed on it. But the banknotes are not exactly alike. Each Bank of England banknote has its own special number, called a **serial number**. No other banknote will have that number.

Earning money

People work to **earn** the money they need. The money they earn is their **income**. There are many ways to earn an income. Some people work in factories or restaurants. Some people build things or drive vehicles. Others take care of ill people or teach in schools.

People can use their education, special skills, or training to work to earn an income.

After working hard, it can feel good to get paid.

An employer pays a person money for the work he or
she does. Some workers still get their pay in the form of
a **cheque**. Many workers choose to let their employer put
their pay directly into the worker's bank account. If you
get paid for doing things like jobs at home or helping
a neighbour, the money you earn is your income.

How money is used

People use the money they **earn** in many ways. They spend some of their **income** on **goods** and **services**. Goods are things people use, like clothes, houses, and toys. Services are things that are done for someone else. For example, people pay waiters, dentists, hairdressers, and vets for the services these workers provide.

People must spend their money wisely, so they have enough to buy the things they really need.

The more money a person earns, the greater the amount of income tax he or she must pay.

Most people save part of their income so they will have money in the future. And many other people give some money away to help others. People must also pay **taxes**. The **government** uses tax money to pay government workers and to build things, such as roads and schools.

Making choices about money

People must use at least part of their income to buy things they need, such as food.

There are many ways to spend money. People use most of their **income** to pay for their needs. These are things they must have, such as food to eat, clothes to wear, and a place to live.

People also spend money on wants. Wants are things they would like to have, but could do without. Televisions, toys, and fancy cars are all wants. How to spend is not the only choice people make about money. They also decide how much to save and how much to give away. If they use their money wisely, they can do some of each.

Many people set aside part of their income to pay for things that are fun, such as sports activities or holidays.

Where money goes

When someone spends money, where does it go? Money travels from person to person and from place to place. The five-pound note used to buy a book today might be in another town by next week. Just follow the journey of this **banknote**.

1 A man gives a shop assistant in Edinburgh a five-pound note to pay for a book.

2 The shop assistant gives the same banknote to a woman as change.

3 The woman puts the same banknote in a birthday card for her nephew.

Money does not last forever. **Coins** get scratched or bent. Paper money gets dirty or torn. But money is not thrown away when it gets old. Coins are melted down at the **Royal Mint** and the metal is used again. Used banknotes are shredded and **recycled**.

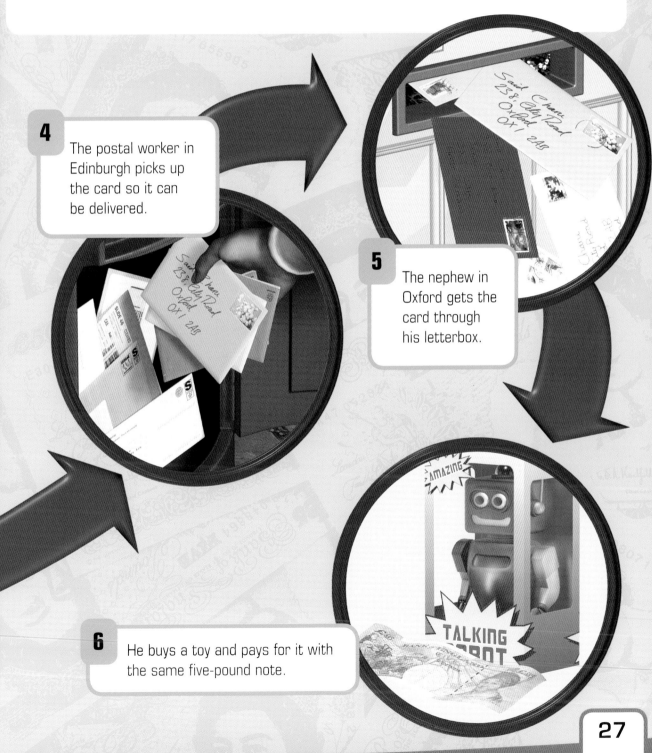

4 The postal worker in Edinburgh picks up the card so it can be delivered.

5 The nephew in Oxford gets the card through his letterbox.

6 He buys a toy and pays for it with the same five-pound note.

Money around the world

The money used in other countries does not look like the money used in the United Kingdom. That is because almost every country has its own money, or **currency**.

Banknotes and coins from different countries do not look the same.

Each currency is different. **Coins** and **banknotes** from different places have different values and usually have different names. The pictures and words that appear on them are not the same either.

People can exchange one currency for
another at a bank or currency exchange.

When people visit other countries, they usually have
to use that country's currency. They can exchange one
currency for the other. Some money can be used in
more than one country. The euro is one kind of currency
that can be used in many different countries in Europe.
Understanding money is important almost everywhere
in the world.

Glossary

Bank of England a special bank. One of its jobs is to issue most of the UK's banknotes. Its main job is to stop prices rising too quickly and it works with other people to keep the banking system working properly.

bank account place where money is kept by a bank on behalf of a customer

banknote paper money

barter to exchange one thing for another without using money

cash coins and paper money

cheque note from the owner of a bank account telling the bank to pay money from their bank account to someone

coin flat piece of metal used as money

currency money used in a certain country or continent

earn to get money by working

employer person or business for whom other people work for pay

goods things people buy, such as food, clothing, and toys

government leaders of a country

income money a person receives from jobs and other sources

Latin language of ancient Rome and its empire. Latin is still taught in many countries.

mint place where coins are made

printing press machine that puts words and pictures onto paper

recycle use again

Royal Mint where coins are made in the United Kingdom

serial number special number used to identify an item

service something done for someone

sterling British money

tax money paid to the government for public services

trade to exchange one thing for another

Index